Original title:
Lyrical Logs

Copyright © 2025 Creative Arts Management OÜ
All rights reserved.

Author: Oliver Bennett
ISBN HARDBACK: 978-1-80567-318-7
ISBN PAPERBACK: 978-1-80567-617-1

Harmonies of the Woodland Whisper

In the woods, the squirrels chatter,
A debate on the best acorn platter.
Frogs leap with lyrical flair,
While owls hoot like a local mayor.

The breeze giggles through the trees,
Tickling leaves with humorous tease.
Nature's jesters play all day,
In their own peculiar way.

Fragments of Evergreen Dreams

A pinecone rolls with style and grace,
Bumping into a raccoon's face.
The chipmunks laugh, it's quite the sight,
As they dance 'neath the moonlight.

A wandering stream sings silly tunes,
While frogs sport hats made of balloons.
Each ripple tells a joke so bright,
In the stillness of the night.

Cadence in the Canopy

Bamboo sways like a funky dancer,
While a woodpecker taps in a merry prancer.
A parrot squawks a cheeky line,
As butterflies tease the sweet sunshine.

The branches sway, they seem to giggle,
At the sight of a rabbit's silly wiggle.
The forest floor is a stage so grand,
Where laughter echoes through the land.

Nature's Narrative in Woodgrain

Trees gossip in their gruff old ways,
Sharing secrets of sunny days.
A bumblebee dons a tiny hat,
Buzzing tunes like a tiny brat.

Logs tell tales of epic fights,
With mischievous sprites in tree-top heights.
Each knot and twist a story to tell,
Of woodland fun that rings a bell.

Verses from the Veiled Vines

In a garden where whispers squawk,
A grape in a hat takes a talk.
It jigs with a carrot, all dressed in green,
Together they plan a dance unseen.

A pumpkin rolls in with a grin so wide,
He's got the best moves and a squashy slide.
The peas start giggling, they can't keep still,
As cucumber joins in, feeling quite chill.

Ballad of the Boughs

The branches hold secrets, oh what a sight,
A squirrel's grand party, it runs through the night.
With acorns as treats and leaves for a hat,
They dance to the rhythm of a charismatic cat.

A robin sings loudly, acting the star,
While a bold little mouse plays an old guitar.
Everyone's laughing, with joy from above,
As nature's own band plays the tune of love.

Notes from the Nurtured Roots

Deep underground chatter, oh what a show,
The carrots sing ballads to the humble potato.
With laughs and with larks, they wiggle in dirt,
As radishes giggle, oh how they hurt!

A wise old turnip shares tales of yore,
About wild cucumber who thought he could soar.
But alas, he just tumbled, rolled over with glee,
Now he's the star of the veggie spree.

Stanzas in the Shade

Under a tree where the shadows play,
A frog plays checkers with a cheeky stray.
The laughter erupts, like bubbles in air,
Where bugs join the fun, with nibbles to share.

A gopher pops out, his hat far too big,
He's got jokes to tell, with a dance and a jig.
As dusk pulls her curtain, the fun doesn't cease,
In this leafy haven, the joy is a feast.

A Symphony Beneath the Leaves

The tree tried to sing, but it just went "crack!"
Squirrels joined in with a nutty little quack.
The birds chimed in, with a chirp and a flap,
While the poor old oak just took a loud nap.

A breeze blew through, playing tunes on the boughs,
Even the daisies danced, making silly vows.
With giggles of grasses, all green and spry,
Every rustle and shuffle made laughter fly by.

Cadences Woven by Nature's Hand

The wind penned a joke on a petal's bright frame,
It whispered so softly, but it sounded the same.
The brook chuckled back with a splash and a gurgle,
While frogs in their croaks formed a comical burble.

The daisies were clappers, oh what a show!
They clinked with a grace, while putting on a glow.
This canvas of sound, painted laughter alive,
In this silly old world, it's a joy to survive.

The Chorus of the Whispering Willows

The willows swayed, singing to each other,
They giggled and swirled like a silly old mother.
Their branches swished whimsically, tickling the air,
As crickets chimed in with their nighttime flair.

One willow turned round with a creaky old sigh,
"Why do we sway? Is it just to comply?"
The answer came back in a rustling rust,
"Because being a tree is a form of pure trust!"

Poetic Reflections of the Riverbank

The river side split with a burst of laughter,
As fish flipped and flopped, with a splash and a chatter.
The stones rolled their eyes, "What a silly old show,"
As turtles grinned wide with nowhere to go.

Rippling, bubbling, the water did tease,
"Catch me if you can!" it called to the breeze.
Together they frolicked, the sun making waves,
In a ballet of glee, with the bubbles as slaves.

The Echoing Heart of the Forest

In the woods where trees wear hats,
Squirrels dance, the birds all chat.
Echoes bounce from bark to leaf,
Nature's gossip, quite the belief.

A chipmunk juggles acorn balls,
Frogs croak jokes from the mossy stalls.
Laughter rings from trunk to sky,
Beneath the branches, time flies high.

Timber Tales of Mystical Lands

Once a tree had quite a dream,
To grow tall and win a meme.
It tried to surf on a squirrel's back,
But tumbled down with quite a whack.

The rabbits cheered, the owls laughed,
As branches joined in, not quite daft.
They spun tall tales of timbered grace,
In a forest fair, a funny place.

The Rhythmic Pulse of the Earth

The ground does jig when creatures prance,
Worms wear boots for a dance.
Beetles marching, kicking dirt,
In this rhythm, no one's hurt.

The grass sings low, the flowers sway,
While ants host parties every day.
With roots that tap their tap-tap tune,
Every trunk sways under the moon.

Whispers Beneath the Bark

In shadows deep where whispers play,
The trees tell tales of yesterday.
A shy oak saw a fox in flight,
And chuckled hard into the night.

With whispers soft, they shared their glee,
As pine cones fell from every tree.
Beneath the bark, the humor flows,
In leafy halls, the laughter grows.

Requiem for the Ringing Cedars

In the forest, trees do sing,
Cedars chime with jokes to bring.
Squirrels giggle, branches sway,
The woodpecker steals the day.

A raccoon dances, oh so sly,
While owls wink, they seem to fly.
The shadows stretch, the sun dips low,
Nature's kung fu, quite the show!

Arboreal Aria

Every leaf has got a tale,
Of birds that sing like a canail.
The acorns tumble, what a sight,
Chasing tails in pure delight.

A cheeky sapling loves to tease,
With whispers carried by the breeze.
The butterflies join in the fun,
Spinning dances 'til they're done.

Cantata of the Creeping Ivy

Ivy creeps with silent grace,
Climbs up walls, a sly embrace.
It whispers jokes to passerby,
As birds fly past with a loud sigh.

The vines form hats on sleeping boughs,
Making nature laugh, oh wow!
Each twist and twirl is full of glee,
As veggied roots join in a spree.

Poetic Pines in the Twilight

Pine trees whisper, tales so tall,
Of chipmunks who think they can ball.
A sunset laugh, a murmur low,
The trees all join in jest, you know!

Each needle pricks at time's own clock,
They chat and giggle, stone-cold rock.
With every breeze, a fresh new pun,
Under the moon, their laughter's spun.

Tales of the Twisting Trails

On a trail where shadows dance,
Lizards waltz in feathered pants.
Squirrels giggle, toss some nuts,
As frogs croak tunes, in silly ruts.

Twisted branches raise a cheer,
Whispering jokes only they hear.
Every path's a comic show,
Nature's laughs put on a glow.

Bumpy roots with winks and grins,
Carry stories of squirrel wins.
Raccoons rhyme in tap-dance fray,
While dandelions join the play.

Roots that Sing of Days Gone By

Beneath the soil, the roots convene,
Whispering tales that are quite serene.
They chatter 'bout the ants so bold,
And worms who wear the shiniest gold.

An oak jokes, "I'm the oldest here,"
A sapling laughs, "You're full of cheer!"
Together they spin yarns to share,
While crickets chirp, "We're a lively pair!"

With every season, a new prank blooms,
As leaves hatch plots in their leafy rooms.
Time ticks slowly, but they won't complain,
For every giggle mutates like rain.

Chords of the Dappled Sunlight

Sunbeams strum on branches high,
Creating melodies that touch the sky.
Shadows wiggle in a playful way,
While beetles join in for a sunny display.

A butterfly yodels, "I'm here to sing!"
As blossoms sway, and the whole world bling.
With daisies clapping, it's quite the sight,
Nature's concert in dazzling light.

The brook bubbles with a bubbling tune,
While frogs audition, hoping to croon.
All around, laughter leads the dance,
In the dappled glow of sweet happenstance.

The Chorus of the Wild Blossoms

In the meadow, the blooms unite,
Swaying lightly in a flower fight.
Petals giggle in colors bright,
As bees compose their buzzing flight.

Daisies declare, "We're the stars!"
While buttercups boast of fancy cars.
The poppies laugh with the sun on their head,
As violets blush from the jokes that are said.

Every sprout in the wild ensemble,
Shares secrets that make the garden tremble.
A floral ruckus, so bright, so grand,
With laughter blooming across the land.

Stanzas of Rustling Foliage

The leaves gossip as they sway,
Telling tales of a windy day.
Squirrels dance on branches high,
While the birds cackle in the sky.

A twig trips up a passing bee,
As it buzzes past, quick as can be.
A rustle here, a chuckle there,
Nature's laughter hangs in the air.

The acorns drop, a clumsy feat,
Dancing underfoot for you to meet.
A gentle breeze sets the show,
With whispers soft and giggles low.

So come and join this leafy spree,
Where laughter blooms like a sunny spree.
In every rustle, there's a song,
Nature's humor all night long.

The Untold Chronicles of Conifers

In the shadows where pine trees sigh,
A secret life goes drifting by.
With needles sharp and cones a-plenty,
These ancient tales, they're quite dainty.

A squirrel wears a cone like a hat,
Strutting proudly, look at that!
While chipmunks throw a tiny bash,
Chasing shadows in a flash.

Breezes bring the whispers low,
Of history only the trees know.
They chuckle softly, sway and lean,
In this festive forest scene.

So listen close, the stories flow,
Of forest friends and their silly show.
Conifers giggle, they can't resist,
In the bark of nature, you can't miss!

Hum of the Tree Canopies

High above where the branches twist,
A chorus forms, you get the gist.
Fluttering leaves hum tunes so sweet,
While critters dance on nimble feet.

A cautious owl blinks with surprise,
As raccoons plot in clever disguise.
A squirrel pipes with a jaunty cheer,
'Come join the fun, there's much to hear!'

Windy whispers and chuckles collide,
Among the branches where secrets hide.
Each rustle a note in this leafy tune,
Under the sun and the watchful moon.

So let's raise a glass to the canopy crew,
Where humor blooms like the morning dew.
In laughter's embrace, let's take a stand,
In this playful orchestra, hand in hand.

Verses of the Wildflower Meadow

In the meadow where colors collide,
Flowers giggle, they cannot hide.
Daisies wink at the passing bee,
While poppies sway so mischievously.

Butterflies flutter in bright array,
Joining the jokes in their own grand play.
Each petal whispers a little jest,
As nature throws her colorful fest.

A bumblebee trips on dewy grass,
Flipping over with style and sass.
The meadow laughs, a joyful delight,
In this kaleidoscope, all feels right.

So skip along this flowery lane,
Where laughter blooms and joy is gain.
In every shade, a smile is found,
In this vibrant patch, love all around.

Elegy of the Engaging Elm

In the park, where branches sway,
An elm tells jokes in a leafy way.
Its bark is rough, but its humor's slick,
Leaves chuckle softly, they're quite the trick.

Squirrels quip about the rainy day,
As acorns scattered, come out to play.
The wind joins in with a breezy cheer,
Who knew trees could lend an ear?

Wisdom flows with a rustling sound,
While passing kids gather around.
The elm stands tall with a grin so wide,
Sharing tales of bark and leaves with pride.

But when night falls and shadows creep,
Its laughter's quiet, like secrets to keep.
Yet if you listen to the rustling this eve,
You'll hear it chuckle, and still believe.

Tales of the Twisting Trails

Down twisting paths where shadows play,
Each turn tells stories in a funny way.
A pine jokes softly with passing ants,
While brambles grin in their leafy pants.

The sunbeams giggle through the trees,
As they dance lightly in the morning breeze.
With flowers nodding beneath their light,
All join in on this silly sight.

Birds chirp puns from heights they claim,
With wings that flutter as if in a game.
Each footstep echoes with laughter anew,
On trails where humor is never through.

Even roots chuckle as they spread wide,
Entwined in stories, they never hide.
So grab your shoes, come join the spree,
For each path leads to joy, you see!

Radiance in the Redwoods

In tall redwoods where sunbeams prance,
Fungi in hats lead a comical dance.
They wiggle their caps with great delight,
As creatures giggle in the soft twilight.

Branches tickle as the wind blows through,
While shadows play peek-a-boo just for you.
A raccoon munches on popcorn, so sly,
While birds quip, 'Did you see him? Oh my!'

Moss-covered rocks add a fuzzy cheer,
While critters convene to share a beer.
With laughter echoing off bark so proud,
These redwoods shine, bright and loud.

At dusk, the giggles merge with the night,
As fireflies blink in a sparkling flight.
In this wonderland where all is bright,
Joy lingers long, 'til morning light.

Dialogue of the Dappled Dawn

As daylight peeks through branches tall,
The morning light starts a playful brawl.
Breezes whisper with a cheeky grin,
Dancing lightly on leaf and skin.

The flowers gossip, colors so bold,
Trading stories of warmth and cold.
With each new bloom comes laughter and cheer,
A riot of color that draws us near.

Sunbeams skip on the waking stream,
While frogs croak jokes in a rhythmic dream.
Each ripple holds a hearty laugh,
Nature's jesters on a playful path.

As shadows stretch and the sun climbs high,
The day unfolds, laughter fills the sky.
In dappled dawn, where joy is spun,
It's hard to tell where the fun is done.

The Living Lyric of the Wilderness

In the woods where squirrels dance,
Bouncing around without a chance.
Raccoons write songs in the night,
While owls hoot, taking flight.

Frogs in chorus croak their tune,
Beneath the watch of the glowing moon.
A deer tries to keep the beat,
While rabbits wiggle their little feet.

The trees sway with the laughter,
Swinging to nature's favorite rafter.
Even the streams hum along,
To the quirky wilderness song.

The Song of Seasons in Shade

In spring, the tulips start to tease,
Blowing kisses in the gentle breeze.
Summer comes with a sassy shout,
As bees decide to dance about.

Autumn brings a playful sight,
Leaves twirling down, oh what a flight!
Winter laughs as snowflakes prance,
Silent, but oh so full of chance.

Each season sings its own bright chime,
Joking with nature, keeping time.
It's a comedy of weather fun,
Where every note is a pun begun.

Sapling Serenades

Tiny sprouts with dreams so tall,
Whisper secrets; they giggle and sprawl.
Wiggly worms tap on the ground,
While ants march, performing unbound.

The saplings sway in the playful breeze,
Waving hello to the buzzing bees.
Sunlight tickles their tender skin,
As they burst forth in a leafy grin.

Every bud is a punchline bright,
In the comedy of green delight.
Roots shout below, 'We are the scene!',
As sprouts burst forth, fresh and keen.

Melodic Murmurs from the Maple

The maple tree hums a silly tune,
Swaying wildly beneath the moon.
Its leaves flap like a helpful hand,
As if to guide a lost little band.

Chirping birds take to the stage,
Singing out as they turn the page.
A woodpecker joins in with a tap,
Creating rhythms that make us clap.

The maple chuckles as the sun shines,
Scratching bark in playful lines.
With each whisper and rustling laugh,
Its trunk tells tales of the earth's craft.

Epic Tales of the Elder Pines

In shadows thick, the stories grow,
Elder pines hum tales we know.
One swayed and slipped, oh what a sight,
A squirrel laughed, it took a flight!

Branches whisper to the breeze,
Pine cones tumble, aimed to tease.
A raccoon snickers, eyes so bright,
Drawing plans for snacks at night!

Mighty trunks with knots and bends,
Compete with tales that never end.
Tree rings count the laughter shared,
In this wood, no heart felt scared!

The elder's bark tells jokes of old,
Wrapped in green, and oh so bold.
If you listen close, you'll hear them call,
"Join our giggle, one and all!"

The Breath of the Birch

Birches sway with a gentle sigh,
Waving to clouds drifting by.
One branch tickles with a funny dance,
While leaves giggle, in a chance romance.

The white bark giggles in the sun,
As beetles march, just for fun.
A woodpecker pecks with a merry thud,
Planting laughter deep in the mud.

Dancing with shadows in the light,
Squirrels joke and take to flight.
"Catch me if you can!" one shouts with glee,
As branches shake like a wild spree!

In the breeze, a chorus sings,
Of whispers brought by playful wings.
A birch tree stands so proud and wide,
With a humor that won't subside!

Rhymes Emanating from the Underbrush

Beneath the ferns, a party brews,
With crickets rapping, sharing news.
Twirling leaves, they spin around,
In this wild, they've truly found.

A rabbit hops, with style and flair,
While hedgehogs snicker at the air.
"Why did the toad cross the way?
To hop on over and play all day!"

The underbrush hums with playful cheer,
As critters gather, drawing near.
Lively banter fills the ground,
In nature's club, joy's always found!

A chipmunk beats a makeshift drum,
While mushrooms nod, saying, "Here comes fun!"
With every rhyme, the forest groans,
In happy tones, they share their bones!

Ode to the Gnarled Roots

Twisted roots in a bendy grace,
Whisper secrets, a secret place.
"Oh, watch your step!" the elder warns,
As giggles bounce through evening's charms.

They tangle with shoes in a playful jest,
Setting traps for the hapless guest.
"Mud on your boots? Just look at us!
We're fashion roots, without a fuss!"

Gnarled and wise, they laugh at fate,
Daring all to join their slate.
"Climb aboard, let's make a mess,
Life's too short, let's not digress!"

Their laughter drifts through the trees,
With snickers carried by the breeze.
So next you stroll, give them a look,
These roots love humor, in every nook!

An Ode to the Green Embrace

When trees wear coats of chartreuse zest,
They tickle the sky, a leafy jest.
Branches wave like wands, oh so slick,
As squirrels plot pranks, clever and quick.

With roots that dance under soil's tight hug,
A trunk like a giant, all warm and snug.
Whispers of jokes carried in the breeze,
Giggles of critters, oh how they tease!

The Silent Symphony of the Strings

The forest hums a tune quite absurd,
With violins played by each little bird.
A bass note thumps from a log on the ground,
While raccoons tap dance in circles around.

Frogs croak along, a comedic voice,
The wind joins in, it has no choice.
Leaves sway to rhythms of laughter and play,
Nature's own band, on a whimsical day.

Tales from the Ancient Timber

Once a tree claimed to be quite the sage,
Spinning wild yarns at every age.
It spoke of clouds, and of raindrops' plight,
And how bees practiced their dance every night.

Knots on its bark tell stories so grand,
Of squirrels in capes and a very brave band.
With each gentle rustle, you hear them cheer,
Legendary pranks that bring hearty cheer.

The Poignant Pulse of Nature's Heart

A thump from the trunk, a heartbeat so sly,
As critters conspire beneath the wide sky.
Bees buzz in rhythm, the sign of the show,
While shadows join in with a soft, funny glow.

The flowers all giggle, their colors parade,
Each blossom a jester, brightly displayed.
With every tickle of wind through the leaves,
Nature laughs hard, no tricks up its sleeves.

Whispers of Waving Woods

In the woods where giggles play,
Trees wear hats in a funny way.
The birch is dancing, swaying free,
Telling jokes to the old pine tree.

Squirrels chuckle, chasing tails,
While deer join in with tiny wails.
A fox tells riddles, oh what fun!
As shadows flicker in the sun.

A woodpecker's tap is quite a tune,
Arguing with a grumpy raccoon.
The owls whisper secrets at night,
With moonlight bringing laughter's delight.

When breezes blow, the leaves all cheer,
As branches sway without a fear.
Nature's stage, a comic spree,
In the woods, so wild and free.

Echoes in the Evergreen

In a forest where laughter grows,
The evergreen wears mismatched clothes.
Hats of moss and scarves of vines,
Tickled trunks in wobbly lines.

A chipmunk juggles acorns round,
While tree frogs croak a merry sound.
The pines hum tunes of olden days,
In this place where humor stays.

A rabbit hops with great delight,
Telling stories until the night.
The shadows dance, the branches lean,
In echoes of the evergreen.

High above, the giggles fly,
As birds share jokes beneath the sky.
In this glade where nature jives,
Funny whispers keep us alive.

The Song of the Sturdy Oak

The sturdy oak sings loud and clear,
With leaves that rustle like a cheer.
Barking dogs join in the fun,
While squirrels race to catch the sun.

Crazy critters in a line,
Twirling round in dance divine.
The oak shakes limbs with every note,
As laughter echoes, wild and rote.

A raccoon plays a tiny drum,
With rabbits bouncing, oh so numb.
Each branch a stage, each root a seat,
Nature's show, a comic treat.

When night falls, the stars all wink,
As tree trunks gather 'round to think.
A concert of both sound and sight,
In the oak's embrace, we find delight.

Rhythms of the Rustling Leaves

Leaves are laughing in the breeze,
Whirling round like happy bees.
The maples dance, the oaks applaud,
As each branch sways, the forest nods.

A gust of wind brings funny tales,
Frogs in tuxedos on sail trails.
An old cat sits with wise old grin,
As nature's laughter flows within.

The twigs tap dance with joyful glee,
While critters play at hide and seek.
With rustling whispers all around,
In leafy laughter, joy is found.

So come and join the playful spree,
In every shade, in every tree.
The rhythms beat, the magic weaves,
In nature's heart, there's fun in leaves.

Words from the Woodland Whisper

In the forest where the trees joke,
Squirrels gather, wearing cloaks.
They hold tea parties with acorn hats,
Trading tales with chattering bats.

Frogs in bow ties croak a sweet tune,
They dance with fireflies under the moon.
A rabbit recites prose of carrot delight,
While hedgehogs groove, oh what a sight!

Owls roll their eyes at the bad puns,
While raccoons eclipse the play with runs.
The forest floor is a stage so grand,
With laughter echoing across the land.

When night falls, all join in the fun,
Stacking mushrooms, they each weigh a ton.
In this wood, life's a merry masquerade,
In laughter and friendship, joy is made.

Canticles of the Climbing Vines

Twisting and winding, the vines take flight,
They wrap around trees, what a silly sight!
They hum tunes with the bees in the air,
Swaying and singing without a care.

Giggling leaves, rustling in glee,
Play hide and seek with the old, wise tree.
A chameleon boasts, 'I can change colors!',
While snails glide by, as slow-paced scholars.

A sloth hangs low, wearing a grin,
"I'm not lazy; I'm conserving my spin!"
Monkeys join in with tricks and jests,
Swinging through branches, they're true jesters' guests.

In this vine-clad realm, laughter flows,
Each twist and turn, more fun it bestows.
A festival of joy, in nature's embrace,
In these climbing trails, forever we chase.

Prose of the Petal Path

On the petal path, where flowers dream,
A daisy whispers, "Life's not as it seems!"
With bees as the audience, they nod their heads,
As tulips tell tales of their colorful spreads.

A sunflower grins, standing so tall,
Claiming, "I'm the king! Come one, come all!"
Yet daisies roll, giggling in play,
"What's a king without a bouquet?"

Butterflies flutter in sparkled delight,
Drinking nectar while avoiding a fight.
Each bloom shares its secrets so sweet,
While grasses sway, casting laughter at their feet.

The path winds onward, a vibrant parade,
In every corner, a joke is displayed.
Here blooms giggle, and petals sing loud,
In this joyful realm, nature's so proud.

Chants of the Cradled Sapling

In the cradle of roots where seedlings giggle,
They share their dreams with a playful wiggle.
"Soon we'll grow tall, just wait and see!"
"Or we might just lie down, sipping sea tea!"

With whispers of wind, the saplings compare,
Who's sprouting fastest? They all declare,
A contest of leaves in the gentle breeze,
While ants parade with unintentional ease.

One, shy and small, hides under a rock,
Telling tall tales while embracing the clock.
Meanwhile, the other insists on grand schemes,
"Climb a mountain or burst into dreams!"

In their cradle, laughter sparks like the sun,
These saplings remind us, life's always fun.
With each little wiggle, a new story begins,
In this charming forest, where friendship wins.

Rhythms Amongst the Roots

Beneath the trees, where shadows dance,
The squirrels gather for their chance.
They tap their feet upon the ground,
While acorns scatter all around.

The roots hum low, a silly tune,
While chipmunks chase the lazy moon.
Each twig and leaf adds to the beat,
In nature's house, we can't be beat.

A rabbit jumps to join the fun,
His tiny feet go thump, thump, run!
With every hop, he shakes the air,
Who knew the forest had such flair?

The sun peeks through, a cheeky grin,
As woodland critters chase their kin.
They share their jokes with every tree,
And laugh together, oh so free!

Serenade of the Old Oak

The old oak sings a song of cheer,
With every branch, it draws us near.
Its leafy crown sways left and right,
Creating music day and night.

With acorns falling like confetti,
The squirrels laugh—oh, aren't they petty!
They hold a feast upon its base,
A nutty gathering with such grace.

A woodpecker adds a tap-tap sound,
As if conducting, all around.
The branches sway in perfect sync,
A concert orchestra on the brink!

The mossy floor becomes a stage,
Where critters dance, forget their age.
In nature's show, we laugh and cheer,
As the old oak plays for all to hear!

Verses Woven in Bark

In the forest where stories grow,
Bark inscribes tales we'll never know.
A squirrel pauses, reads with glee,
While birds scribble their songs in decree.

The logs are stacked like happy pies,
With owls hooting their silly lies.
Each line is marked with rough and smooth,
A funny rhythm that finds its groove.

A raccoon juggles twigs with flair,
As laughter echoes through the air.
The wise old trees chuckle a bit,
At the antics of the furry wit.

So here in woods where laughter rings,
The verses come on playful wings.
Each bark a line, a tale in rhyme,
In every nook, the fun's sublime!

Harmonic Trunks and Twisted Vines

Twisted vines hang like a band,
Making melodies on demand.
The trunks sway gently, side to side,
As if they're all on a goofy ride.

A playful breeze sings through the leaves,
And every critter just believes.
That nature has a sense of fun,
With every twist, a race begun.

Logs play percussion, roots keep time,
While critters dance in perfect rhyme.
A whimsical concert under sun,
Where laughter echoes, never done.

So come and join this lovely spree,
Amongst the trunks, wild and free.
With nature's band, we'll sing and cheer,
In this merry woodland atmosphere!

Odes to the Old Growth

In the forest, giants stand,
With beards of moss, so grand.
Whispers of the woodpecker's song,
They chuckle as I jog along.

Branches stretching, reaching high,
One tips its hat to the sky.
Roots that trip the unsuspecting,
Nature's laughter, quite reflecting.

Fallen logs, they tell a tale,
Of squirrel chases, wild and frail.
A riddle carved in bark tonight,
Who knew trees could be such a sight?

Oh old growth, with stories vast,
From baby birds to shadows cast.
You sway, you giggle, you maybe tease,
Nature's comedians, if you please.

Tones of Timber and Twilight

In twilight's glow, the lumber sings,
A chorus found where laughter clings.
The oak cracks jokes with the willow breeze,
And pine tree puns bring us to our knees.

With every creak of sturdy wood,
A punchline strikes like it once stood.
Logs collide, in playful jest,
Elder trees just paint the best.

Maples wink, their leaves a-flutter,
Whispering sweet, silly mutter.
Even the stumps get in on the game,
Growing a giggle, not just a name.

Oh timber tones that twine and glide,
In this laughing glade, we all abide.
Where twilight shines on bark and bloom,
Nature's humor fills every room.

The Tranquil Treetops

Above, where breezes play a tune,
The treetops sway beneath the moon.
With nests of laughter perched on high,
Curious owls tell jokes that fly.

A sloth so slow, he takes his time,
While squirrels dance in perfect rhyme.
With acorns tossed and giggles shared,
In peaceful heights, we're all ensnared.

A canopy of humor bright,
Where sunlight plays in dappled light.
Leaves rustle secrets, oh so sly,
The treetops jest as time sweeps by.

In tranquil bliss, the world feels right,
As nature's glee ignites the night.
We swing and sway in joyful glee,
For up in the trees, we're wild and free.

Sonnet of the Swaying Sycamore

A sycamore sways with a charming grin,
Telling tales of the storms it has braved.
Its roots' embrace, a ticklish din,
While breezes tease, it giggles and waved.

Birds perch upon, with jokes to share,
Each fluttering laugh a note on the air.
As branches bend, they spin and twirl,
In this comedic world, we're lost in whirl.

With every rustle, a punchline spoken,
The bark holds secrets, never broken.
Fluffy clouds drift, wild like a pack,
This sycamore's jest brings all laughter back.

Under its shade, we find our cheer,
For life's a play, and the trees know here.

Ballads in the Brambles

In the thicket where the bramble sings,
A hedgehog jigs, and a rabbit springs.
Dancing leaves tickle the sunlit dew,
While a lizard croons just for you.

The fox in a hat prances all around,
His shadow dances, up, then down.
Berries burst with a juicy cheer,
As squirrels giggle, 'Come join us here!'

Each thump-a-thump leads to a twirl,
Watch out for the whirl of that dancing squirrel!
Twigs tap out beats in a merry trance,
To a woodland jig, we all must dance!

So gather round, for the woodland show,
With pinecone pomp and acorn flow.
A song for all in the brushy nooks,
In the bramble ballads, let's write the books!

Trills of the Treetops

Up in the branches, laughter flies,
With parrots plotting their silly ties.
The old owl snores, while the woodpecker plays,
An offbeat ruckus that sways and sways.

A squirrel composes with a nutty flair,
While the rabbits raise tunes with a twitch of their hair.
The sunbeams wink, and the breezes sigh,
As ferns join in, waving hello to the sky!

A cacophony echoes through green and brown,
As creatures all work to throw a grand crown.
Twigs wrap up beats, the leaves sing along,
In the trills of treetops, we all belong!

So hoot, chirp, and flap with delightful glee,
In a chorus of mischief, come dance with me!
Up in the canopy, where the laughter flows,
The treetops ring out, as everybody knows!

The Melody of Misty Mornings

With whispers of fog, the morning creeps,
A raccoon in slippers stumbles and leaps.
The sun yawns wide, with a sleepy glow,
As frogs play notes in a soggy show.

Caterpillars crawl, doing the twist,
While a sleepy owl won't get the gist.
Grasshoppers hop like they own the day,
Frolicking in fog, in a hazy ballet!

The brook babbles softly, telling its tales,
As beavers chortle, weaving their sails.
In hues of mist, the world's alive,
With each croak and sigh, fresh laughter will thrive!

So if you hear giggles and splashes near,
It's just morning's music, nothing to fear.
In the melody of mornings misty and bright,
Join the animals in their song of delight!

Verses on the Wilderness Wind

Oh, the wind carries secrets on whistling trails,
Where turtles wear glasses and tell winning tales.
The cactus on wheels rolls through the sand,
Yelling out cheers to the driftwood band.

The breeze swirls around with a whoosh and a whirl,
Making leaves dance, giving nature a twirl.
An old gnome chuckles, tipping his hat,
To the chorus of crickets, a merry chat!

The sun steps in, casting shadows that prance,
While mice in a conga-line join in the dance.
With verses that float, like clouds on the breeze,
All creatures rejoice, with giggles and ease!

So let's spin with joy in the wilderness wide,
Where giggles and chuckles will always abide.
With the wind as our guide, we'll laugh till we drop,
In the whimsical world where the fun never stops!

Harmonies of the Hidden Thicket

In the thicket, squirrels prance,
They wear tiny hats and dance.
With acorns they play a silly tune,
While the moon giggles, making them swoon.

A hedgehog claims he's a rock star,
With prickles that shine from afar.
He strums on blades of grass with glee,
His fans cheer loud, just wait and see!

The owls hoot jokes, oh so wise,
While rabbits giggle, rolling their eyes.
A chorus of crickets keeps time,
Each chirp a punchline, oh so prime!

The thicket comes alive by night,
Under twinkling stars, such a sight.
Nature's laughter fills the air,
In this realm of joy without a care.

Reverberations of the Rich Earth

The ground shakes with a friendly cheer,
As worms tell tales that all can hear.
With rumbles and grumbles, they spin their yarns,
For every burrow, laughter adorns.

The roots below form a band so tight,
With fungi jamming, it's quite a sight.
The thump of tubers, a beat so round,
The fun never stops where friends are found.

Acorns drop with a plop and a thud,
Rolling away like a little mud.
Each bump is a giggle, each fall a joke,
While mushrooms chuckle as they go up in smoke.

The earth is alive with antics galore,
With sprouting laughter that we adore.
Underneath, there's a party so fine,
In the rich soil where the critters dine!

Melodies of the Forest Floor

The forest floor hums a silly tune,
With mushrooms dancing beneath the moon.
Dancing dry leaves swirl up high,
While crickets play, "Don't be shy!"

Frogs croak out the latest trend,
With polka dots they're keen to send.
Tucked in moss, a fox pranks a hare,
Catch me if you can, but beware!

A ladybug brings the beatbox vibe,
While caterpillars do the jive.
Each step creates a musical note,
As the ants march and tap, they gloat!

In sneaky shadows, laughter thrives,
This forest floor where joy arrives.
Amidst the roots and twigs galore,
A raucous symphony forever in store.

Whispered Echoes in Timber

The tall trees whisper secrets and jokes,
With giggles that shake their sturdy oaks.
Branches sway, stars wink and chuckle,
As the moon shines bright, giving a snuggle.

A woodpecker drumming a humorous beat,
Says, "Knock, knock!" to everyone he meets.
The echoes bounce off bark and leaves,
As creatures below share what they believe.

The chipmunk slips, nearly trips on a log,
He laughs it off, "Just a dance from the fog!"
In every hollow, a chuckle can be found,
As timbered laughter fills up the ground.

Midst the trees, the stories unwind,
In wooden tones, a raucous kind.
Whispers and giggles flow with grace,
In the timbered world, it's a merry place.

Melodies Beneath the Bark

In the woods where whispers play,
Squirrels dance and chirp all day.
Branches sway with laughter bright,
Carrying tunes both day and night.

Frogs compose their lovely croak,
While owls recite a silly joke.
Leaves rustle like a jolly choir,
Igniting joy, setting hearts afire.

Rabbits groove on grassy floors,
Skunks parade and share their roars.
A symphony of silly sights,
Nature's concert, pure delights.

So here we join the frolic spree,
In melody of tree and bee.
Where laughter echoes, joy runs free,
Beneath the boughs, come sing with me!

Serenade of the Silver Birch

Oh silver birch with bark so bright,
You tickle clouds, the birds take flight.
Your branches sway in cheerful tone,
With every twist, you dance alone.

Funny bugs parade in line,
Each one dressed in colors fine.
The breeze hums tunes, a dandy beat,
While little critters stamp their feet.

Beneath your shade, the squirrels play,
They crack their jokes and hip-hip-hey!
Twisted roots form a wobbly stage,
For woodland mischief, all the rage!

Oh silver queen of nature's floor,
You bring us laughter, want more, more!
In your embrace, we find our glee,
A serenade of ecstasy!

Chronicles of the Charmed Canopy

In the canopy, antics unfold,
From squeezably soft to delightfully bold.
A chitter-chatter of feathery friends,
With tales of trouble that never ends.

A hedgehog rolls with giggly flair,
Declared a knight in leafy wear.
The owls hoot jokes about the time,
A raccoon tried to climb a vine!

The breezes lull with whimsy's sigh,
As butterflies twirl and glide on high.
Each leaf tells tales of laughter shared,
Where joy and silliness are declared.

So join the dance beneath the trees,
Where funny tales float on the breeze.
Chronicles spun by heart and mind,
In this enchanted place, joy we find!

Hymns of the Hidden Hollow

In the hidden hollow, sounds arise,
Where every rustle wears a guise.
Beneath the ferns, the giggles grow,
As critters hum their secret show.

A plump raccoon, with mischief rife,
Steals a snack of woodland life.
The tall trees sway, they know the tune,
Singing softly under the moon.

Fireflies blink like nature's lights,
Hosting parties in starry nights.
With goofy grins, the creatures gleam,
In a hollow where laughter beams.

Join the hymn of our hidden place,
With squirrelly steps that set the pace.
In this realm of whimsy and cheer,
Every moment is pure and dear!

Rhymes in the Rustic Clarity

In the woods where squirrels dance,
A rabbit tried to wear my pants.
He hopped and twirled with great delight,
But tripped on roots and took to flight.

The hedgehogs threw a cozy feast,
With acorns lined from west to east.
They laughed at me, I tried to sing,
But ended up with quite the sting.

An owl hooted, quite a prank,
As I tripped over a muddy bank.
The frogs all croaked, they joined the game,
While fireflies lit up the frame.

So here's to fun amidst the trees,
Where nature brings such jolly pleas.
With every step, a humorous slip,
In this woodland, I find my grip.

A Tapestry of Leafy Lyrics

A squirrel wore a tiny hat,
Demanding snacks, imagine that!
The birds just giggled, flew in queues,
While I was stuck in muddy shoes.

A bear appeared with honeyed paws,
Inviting all to join his cause.
He said, "Don't worry, it's just a snack,"
But ended up with ants on his back!

The flowers swayed, they felt the beat,
As dancing ants skipped 'neath my feet.
In laughter's grip, we spun around,
Creating melodies from the ground.

With whispers sweet and puns so spry,
The forest echoed every sigh.
A tapestry of sounds we weave,
In this quirky world, I believe!

The Unseen Echo in the Glen

In the glen where shadows roll,
A cricket played the leading role.
His concert reached the stars so bright,
But lost the tune and took to flight!

The trees all burst with laughter grand,
As the wind blew through, its mischievous hand.
A raccoon danced, not quite in time,
He stepped on leaves, it sounded prime!

The echoes bounced from tree to tree,
A symphony of hilarity.
Each snap and crack brought joy so pure,
As critters joined in for a cure.

So let the unseen whispers play,
In this delightful, funny way.
The glen alive with joy and noise,
Where nature sings with giddy poise.

Whispers of Woodland Wonders

A squirrel told me quite a tale,
Of how he rode a tiny snail.
He laughed and flipped from tree to tree,
While deer just stared, bewildered, see!

The bunnies jumped, they formed a line,
In synchronized moves, oh so fine.
But tripped on clover, landed flat,
In stitches now, they laughed at that!

A fox with style, in shades so bright,
Claimed he'd challenge any sight.
But slipped on dew, oh what a sight,
He rolled away, a furry light!

So here in woods where laughter gleams,
We weave our tales, fulfill our dreams.
With every twist and turn we find,
Woodland wonders, humor entwined.

Reflections Among the Ferns

In ferns so green, my thoughts take flight,
A squirrel scurries, what a sight!
He steals my snack, a daring crime,
I laugh as he runs, oh how sublime!

The mushrooms dance in tiny shoes,
Their caps a shade of bright chartreuse.
The hedgehog giggles, quite unsure,
Of all the gossip whispered here, for sure.

The sun peeks through, a cheeky grin,
The shadows laugh, let the games begin!
With every rustle, secrets play,
In this wild world, I'll lose my way.

Yet here I sit, a giddy fool,
With nature's charm, I've found my school.
A lesson learned without a book,
In ferns I find my favorite nook.

The Wooded Whisper's Verse

In the woods where whispers live,
The trees exchange what they can give.
A raccoon winks, oh what a rogue,
He steals my hat, I'm in a choke!

The path is paved with acorn dreams,
Where sunlight spills in golden beams.
An owl swoops down, with flair and twist,
"Mind the puns!" he hoots, as I insist.

The breeze, it teases with gentle tickles,
While chipmunks rush with little giggles.
They scurry quick, they know the score,
In nature's jest, who could ask for more?

With every step, I ballet dance,
Each leaf a partner, take a chance.
As laughter echoes through the trees,
The woods are full of silly ease.

The Chronicles of the Stillness

In quiet glades where silence reigns,
A frog sings loud and breaks the chains.
His croaks resound, a concert grand,
The crickets join, it's quite the band!

The deer, they pause, with puzzled looks,
As if to read from ancient books.
They nod along, a silent cheer,
In nature's play, they hold me near.

The stillness hums a tune so sly,
While butterflies and hawks swoop by.
With laughter woven in the air,
This quietude becomes a fair.

So here I sit, a jovial elf,
Riding on whims, just being myself.
As stories swirl in cloaked disguise,
Nature conspires with joyful sighs.

Stanzas in Shaded Light

In shadows cast by trees so tall,
A playful breeze begins to call.
The sun peeks through, a golden ray,
A game of hide and seek at play.

The ants parade in lines so straight,
With tiny banners, they celebrate.
A caterpillar joins the line,
Wobbling here, it's quite divine!

The dappled light creates a stage,
For all the critters to engage.
A cricket plays an amusing tune,
While moles juggle below the moon.

With laughter echoing all around,
In shaded light, pure joy is found.
I dance among the leafy sights,
Where every moment ignites delights.

Chants Beneath Canopy

Under the leaves, where the critters play,
A squirrel hollers, "Hey, it's a sunny day!"
The roots start to giggle, all twisted and spry,
While the branches whisper, "Look, there goes a fly!"

The shadows dance lightly, in breezy delight,
A raccoon in shades claims the afternoon light.
With acorns as maracas, they make quite the sound,
Nature's own band, where the laughter is found.

Songs of the Silent Saplings

Tiny green whispers in a row they stand,
With leaves like a chorus, they sway hand in hand.
Pinecones drop rhythm, like raindrops in June,
The bark holds the secrets, sings softly to the moon.

Each sprout tells a story, a tale spun from light,
Of kernel-filled dreams on a starry night.
They sway to the jest of an invisible breeze,
These pint-sized performers with trunks like a tease!

Ballad of the Wind-Worn Willow

A willow wore glasses, slightly askew,
With a grin that said, "I've seen just about you!"
It fluffed up its branches, preparing for fun,
And invited a picnic—everyone run!

The breeze played a tune through its wispy hair,
While the sun joined the party, oh what a fair!
With laughter and shadows, they twirled in delight,
That wind-worn old willow was quite the invite!

Notes from the Hollowed Heart

In a tree-diagram of laughs and of grins,
A hollowed-out trunk keeps the joy that it spins.
Dust bunnies giggle in their cozy little bed,
As the branches hang low, scratching each other's head.

The woodpecker taps out a cheeky old tune,
Underneath this grand roof, life feels like a boon.
With echoes of chuckles, the forest's in stitches,
Growing older together, through all life's little hitches.

Echoes from the Elder Tree

In a tree so old and wise,
Squirrels plot to organize.
Wily winds whisper in tune,
Awakening sleep with a swoon.

Branches croon a quirky song,
Where acorns dance all day long.
Tangled roots with secrets keep,
While owls chuckle just asleep.

Raccoons lead a midnight show,
With moonlight guiding them to glow.
All the critters join in cheer,
In this forest, all's sincere.

Every branch and leaf agrees,
Nature's quirks bring us to tease.
Elder Tree, we laugh and swing,
Life's such fun; let the woodlands sing!

Songs of the Sunlit Glade

In glades where sunlight beams and plays,
Frogs croon silly tunes all day,
Flowers sway to the rhythm's beat,
While bees buzz on their tiny feet.

A sunny frog in a coat so dapper,
Jumps high like a little hapless capper.
His friends cheer, what a sight to see,
A showdown of wits, just wait and be.

Grasshoppers giggle as they hop,
While daisies throw a lollipop.
Nature's laughter echoes through,
In this glade, nothing's amiss, it's true.

The sun sets low, the giggles rise,
With fireflies twinkling in the skies.
Together they twist, twirl, and sashay,
In the golden light where we all play!

The Timbre of the Twilight Thicket

In twilight's embrace, soft sounds abound,
Woodland whispers swirl all around.
A thrush sings tales of mismatched shoes,
Making friends with giggling blues.

Crickets snap their fingers right,
As nighttime paints the world with light.
Furry critters come to join,
The antics roll, oh what a coin!

Beneath the stars, the night unfolds,
Stories of mischief, silly golds.
Wolves chuckle, their humor slick,
In shadows, laughter takes a pick.

Amongst the trees, pure fun ignites,
Twilight thickets bring playful sights.
With every note the forest hums,
We laugh until the morning comes!

Harmonies of Hidden Hollows

In hidden hollows, secrets lie,
Rabbits whisper and ducks fly by,
Echoes ripple, giggles ring,
Blending sounds that the forest brings.

Daring mice in tiny hats,
Twirl and spin with little chats.
Chipmunks join, leap up and down,
In a swirling jest, they twirl and clown.

Wishing on stars, they tumble through,
Under the gaze of a moonlight blue.
Dreams waltz softly in the cool night air,
While shadows dance with playful flair.

This harmony of creatures small,
Draws the magic; the fun to all.
In hidden hollows, joy's unfurled,
A symphony of laughter to the world!

www.ingramcontent.com/pod-product-compliance
Lightning Source LLC
Chambersburg PA
CBHW072144200426
43209CB00051B/389